ON THE JOB

Creative Careers

Be an ARCHITECT!

Theresa Emminizer

PowerKiDS press

Published in 2025 by The Rosen Publishing Group, Inc.
2544 Clinton Street, Buffalo, NY 14224

First Edition

Editor: Theresa Emminizer
Book Design: Michael Flynn

Photo Credits: Cover Rawpixel.com/Shutterstock.com; (series background) KanokpolTokumhnerd/Shutterstock.com; (series boxes) vector illustration/Shutterstock.com; p. 5 DoublePHOTO studio/Shutterstock.com; p. 7 stockelements/Shutterstock.com; p. 9 Carlos Bruzos Valin/Shutterstock.com; p. 11 (main) Elnur/Shutterstock.com; p. 11 (inset) Kosoff/Shutterstock.com; p. 13 Owlie Productions/Shutterstock.com; p. 15 DC Studio/Shutterstock.com; p. 17 Gorodenkoff/Shutterstock.com; p. 19 Media_Photos/Shutterstock.com; p. 21 Krakenimages.com/Shutterstock.com; p. 23 (left) Hayk_Shalunts/Shutterstock.com; p. 23 (middle) EQRoy/Shutterstock.com; p. 23 (right) Vlas Telino studio/Shutterstock.com; p. 25 UladzimirZuyeu/Shutterstock.com; p. 27 Ritu Manoj Jethani/Shutterstock.com; p. 29 U. J. Alexander/Shutterstock.com.

Cataloging-in-Publication Data

Names: Emminizer, Theresa.
Title: Be an architect! / Theresa Emminizer.
Description: Buffalo, NY : PowerKids Press, 2025. | Series: On the job: creative careers | Includes glossary and index.
Identifiers: ISBN 9781499449549 (pbk.) | ISBN 9781499449556 (library bound) | ISBN 9781499449563 (ebook)
Subjects: LCSH: Architecture–Vocational guidance–Juvenile literature.
Classification: LCC NA1995.E49 2025 | DDC 720–dc23

Manufactured in the United States of America

Some of the images in this book illustrate individuals who are models. The depictions do not imply actual situations or events.

CPSIA Compliance Information: Batch #CWPK25. For Further Information contact Rosen Publishing at 1-800-237-9932.

CONTENTS

THE BEAUTY OF BUILDINGS

The next time you step outside, take a look around you. Notice the shapes and forms of the buildings you see. What draws your eye? Is it a tall, angular skyscraper? A curvy modern structure? Or an old-fashioned church? Have you ever wondered who designed the buildings that surround you? Who built your home, your school, or the buildings where you spend your life? Architects did!

Architecture is the art of designing buildings. People who practice architecture are called architects. Architects use their creativity to design, plan, and construct buildings that are not only pleasing to look at, but also safe and functional, or usable.

Whether you live in a big city or a small town, architecture is all around you.

ARCHITECTS IN ACTION

Architects design all sorts of buildings: skyscrapers, houses, schools, hospitals, libraries, and more! The different types of architecture are based on the purpose of the structures being built.

- Commercial architects design places where things are bought and sold, or work is done, such as offices, stores, and hotels.
- Industrial architects design factories and warehouses.
- Residential architects design homes and places for people to live.
- Sustainable architects are sometimes called green architects. They make eco-friendly, or earth-friendly, designs.
- Urban designers plan how urban, or city, spaces are laid out and design public spaces.

LEARNING ON THE JOB!

Norman Foster is an English architect whose work overlaps different types of architecture. His work includes the Hong Kong International Airport, the Millenium Bridge in London, and the Millau Viaduct in France. A viaduct is a bridge that's often long, high, and carries a railroad or road over something.

Norman Foster designed Hearst Tower in New York City, a commercial building that's a masterpiece of sustainable architecture.

STYLES AND MOVEMENTS

Just as there are different kinds of architects, there are different architectural styles. A period in which certain styles and ideas are popular is called a movement. Some movements overlap. Today's architecture is **influenced** by earlier styles and movements.

A Brief Timeline of Architectural Movements

7th to 4th century BCE	Classic
1050 CE to 1170 CE	Romanesque
1100 CE to 1450 CE	Gothic
1400 CE to 1600 CE	Renaissance
1600 CE to 1755 CE	Baroque
1750 CE to 1920 CE	NeoClassical
1925	Art Deco
1917 to 1965	Modernism
1950 to 2007	Post Modernism
1997-Present	Parametricism

LEARNING ON THE JOB!

Architectural movements show us what was important to people during certain times. Styles continue to be used and referenced, or talked about long after a movement ends.

Similar shapes, colors, and **motifs** can be seen across different architectural works during a movement.

METHODS AND MATERIALS

During each movement, architects use particular methods and materials, or building items, to create their work.

Frank Lloyd Wright was a celebrated American architect who designed more than 1,000 buildings in his lifetime. Part of the modernist movement, Wright specialized in designing homes that blended in with natural surroundings. To do this, he often used native materials, such as stone and wood, alongside modern materials such as steel.

Zaha Hadid was a British-Iraqi architect who led the parametricism movement. Parametricism features algorithmic design, or the use of math to create non-traditional forms. Hadid is nicknamed "the queen of the curve" because her designs break from traditional linear forms.

LEARNING ON THE JOB!

Architects like Wright and Hadid chose their methods and materials based on larger creative visions, or ideas. They were pioneers, or leaders, who **inspired** others.

Fallingwater

Aliyev Center

Wright's Fallingwater is a house built over a waterfall, featuring natural rock. Hadid's Heydar Aliyev Center shows her curvy, non-traditional designs.

FROM MIND TO MATTER

No matter what kind of architecture is being designed, the architectural process can be simplified into seven main phases, or steps.

- Pre-design: Architects talk to **clients** about their wishes. They gather information, or facts, about the site and building rules. They brainstorm ideas.
- Schematic Design: The architect sketches, or draws, a design.
- Design Development: The plan becomes more detailed, or involved. Materials are chosen. A cost statement is made.
- Construction Documents: The plan is finalized and working construction drawings are made.
- Building Permit: The building **authority** approves, or passes, the design.
- Bidding and Negotiation: Architects find a contractor to **execute** their design.
- Construction Administration: Architects oversee construction.

LEARNING ON THE JOB!

Architects work closely with engineers and contractors. A structural engineer's job is to make sure that a building is sound. A contractor's job is to build things.

WHAT IT TAKES

As the seven-step process shows, architects have a wide range of tasks and responsibilities. They must be more than creative visionaries. They need to have a great knowledge of math and science. They need to understand building materials and construction methods. They need to be aware of building codes, or rules.

During each step of the process, architects need to be able to solve problems and think of new ways of doing things. They need to be able to communicate clearly and work well with others. They also need to work within a certain budget, or amount of money to complete a project. They need to be able to meet deadlines too.

Architecture isn't easy! There are many elements to keep in mind.

EDUCATION

To become an architect, one must earn a degree from an architecture school. The school must be approved by the National Architecture **Accrediting** Board (NAAB). Architects need at least a five-year undergraduate degree in architecture known as a B.Arch. While earning their B.Arch, students study architecture techniques and learn about building codes. Some students continue their education in a master's program known as an M.Arch. An M.Arch takes another two or three years to complete.

After completing a B.Arch, **aspiring** architects in the United States can take a test called the Architect Registration Examination (ARE). Architects can only become **licensed** and practice architecture if they have passed all six parts of the ARE.

Before choosing a college or university, it's important to make sure that its architecture program is accredited by the NAAB.

LEARNING ON THE JOB!

There are some four-year Bachelor of Architecture degrees, but they aren't usually approved by the NAAB. Students who earn four-year degrees may need to add an M.Arch later.

EXPERIENCE

It's important for aspiring architects to gain practical, or hands-on, experience. Taking on an internship is a great way to get started! An internship is a temporary, or short-term, work experience in which a student or beginner can learn about a field from a **professional**. Internships are sometimes part of a student's undergraduate program.

Interns get to see firsthand how professional architects work. They get to contribute to projects and get a sense of how each step of the architectural process is completed. An internship helps a student shift from school into real work. Top architecture firms such as Gensler, Perkins&Will, and HDR offer internships.

LEARNING ON THE JOB!

The Architectural Experience Program (AXP) is a program that helps aspiring architects build and track their real-world experience. Architects usually need to complete the AXP to get licensed.

Internships help beginners build connections with other people in their field.

LICENSURE

To practice architecture, you must become licensed in your jurisdiction. A jurisdiction is the region, or area, where you'll be practicing. There are 55 jurisdictions in the United States. The rules and requirements of each jurisdiction are slightly different. Each has its own licensing board, which must approve an architect's **application**. Most jurisdictions require that an architect has:

- A B.Arch and/or M.Arch from an NAAB-accredited program.
- Experience through the AXP or other hands-on work.
- Passed all six parts of the ARE.

Some jurisdictions require architects to pass another test that shows they have knowledge about the particular area of architecture they'll practice in.

Congratulations! Having your license means you can finally call yourself an architect!

SCHEDULE AND LIFESTYLE

What kind of environments, or places, do architects work in? Architects may work in large architectural firms, medium-sized practices, or small **studios**. Architects usually work in offices. Some even work from home! They spend a lot of time working on computers, however they often need to meet and talk with clients and coworkers. Architects also spend time at building sites, thinking about ideas and overseeing the construction of their designs.

Most architects work about 40 hours a week, but may work more when drawing close to a deadline. Architects have many responsibilities, which means their work is often stressful, or trying.

LEARNING ON THE JOB!

Some architects travel internationally, or around the world! Frank Gehry is an American architect whose work can be seen in several different countries.

Walt Disney Concert Hall

Louis Vuitton Foundation

Dancing House

Frank Gehry's work includes the Walt Disney Concert Hall in Los Angeles, the Louis Vuitton Foundation in Paris, and the Dancing House in Prague!

SALARY

A salary is the amount of money someone earns for doing a job. Architects' salaries differ greatly based on the amount of experience they have, what kind of business they work for, and their licensure. The median salary of U.S. architects is about $93,310--this means half of all salaries are higher and half are lower.

Architecture jobs are expected to grow by about 5 percent in the next ten years. California, District of Columbia, New Jersey, and Nevada are some of the best-paying states for architects to practice. Architects work closely with engineers, contractors, and other professionals. Check out the chart on page 25 to see how their salaries compare.

Architecture and Related Jobs

JOBS	MEDIAN SALARY
Architects	$93,310
Architectural and Engineering Managers	$165,370
Civil Engineers	$95,890
Construction Managers	$104,900
Landscape Architects	$79,320
Urban Planners	$81,800

Although these professionals often work together on projects, their salaries are different.

ARCHITECTURAL AWARDS

Great architects can hope to earn more than a good living. Architectural awards and honors are given to the best and brightest creators in the field. The American Institute of Architects (AIA) gives out awards based on different **categories** of work, including the Young Architects Award, the Housing Awards, and many others.

There are also many international awards for architectural excellence. The Pritzker Prize is thought of as the highest of all architecture awards. Each year, it's awarded to an architect to honor and celebrate their life's work. Philip C. Johnson, Kevin Roche, I.M. Pei, Thom Mayne, Robert Venturi, Richard Meier, and Gordon Bunshaft are American architects who have won the Pritzker Prize.

Philip C. Johnson was the first winner of the Pritzker Prize in 1979. Johnson designed the Glass House (pictured here), in New Canaan, Connecticut.

DO YOU WANT TO BE AN ARCHITECT?

The path to becoming an architect is long and hard. Architects must work through years of education, on-the-job training, and challenging testing before they can even earn their license! More than that, they must have a unique, or one-of-a-kind, vision that sets them apart from the crowd and helps them create eye-catching and functional art.

Does the world of architecture excite you? You don't have to wait to earn your B.Arch to get started! Draw pictures of the designs in your mind! Play with Legos or build a fort! Check out pictures of great architectural works and find out more about pioneers who created them and the movements that inspired them.

An architect's mind is their most powerful tool.
What creations can you imagine?

GLOSSARY

accredit: To give official approval to someone who has met a set of standards.

application: A request for a job or admittance to a school.

aspiring: Strongly wanting to achieve a goal.

authority: The person or group with the power to give orders or make decisions.

category: A group of things that are in some certain way similar.

client: Someone who pays a professional for a certain service.

execute: To carry out or put something, such as a plan, into effect.

influence: An effect one thing has on another.

inspire: To move someone to do something.

licensed: Having legal permission to do something.

motif: A repeated pattern, image, or theme.

professional: Someone who does a certain job for a living. Also, having to do with a job someone does for a living.

studio: A building or room where an artist or artists work.

FOR MORE INFORMATION

BOOKS

Markovics, Joyce L. *Smart Architecture*. Ann Arbor, Michigan: Cherry Lake Publishing, 2023.

Mulder-Slater, Andrea, Geoff Slater, and Jantje Blokhuis-Mulder. *Awesome Architecture Activities for Kids*. Emeryville, CA: Rockridge Press, 2023.

WEBSITES

archKIDecture
archkidecture.org/projects-and-lessons/
Try out these fun architecture projects at home!

The Kids Should See This
thekidshouldseethis.com/tagged/architecture
Check out awesome videos about how to experiment with architecture and learn more about it.

Publisher's note to educators and parents: Our editors have carefully reviewed these websites to ensure that they are suitable for students. Many websites change frequently, however, and we cannot guarantee that a site's future contents will continue to meet our high standards of quality and educational value. Be advised that students should be closely supervised whenever they access the internet.

INDEX